I0605858

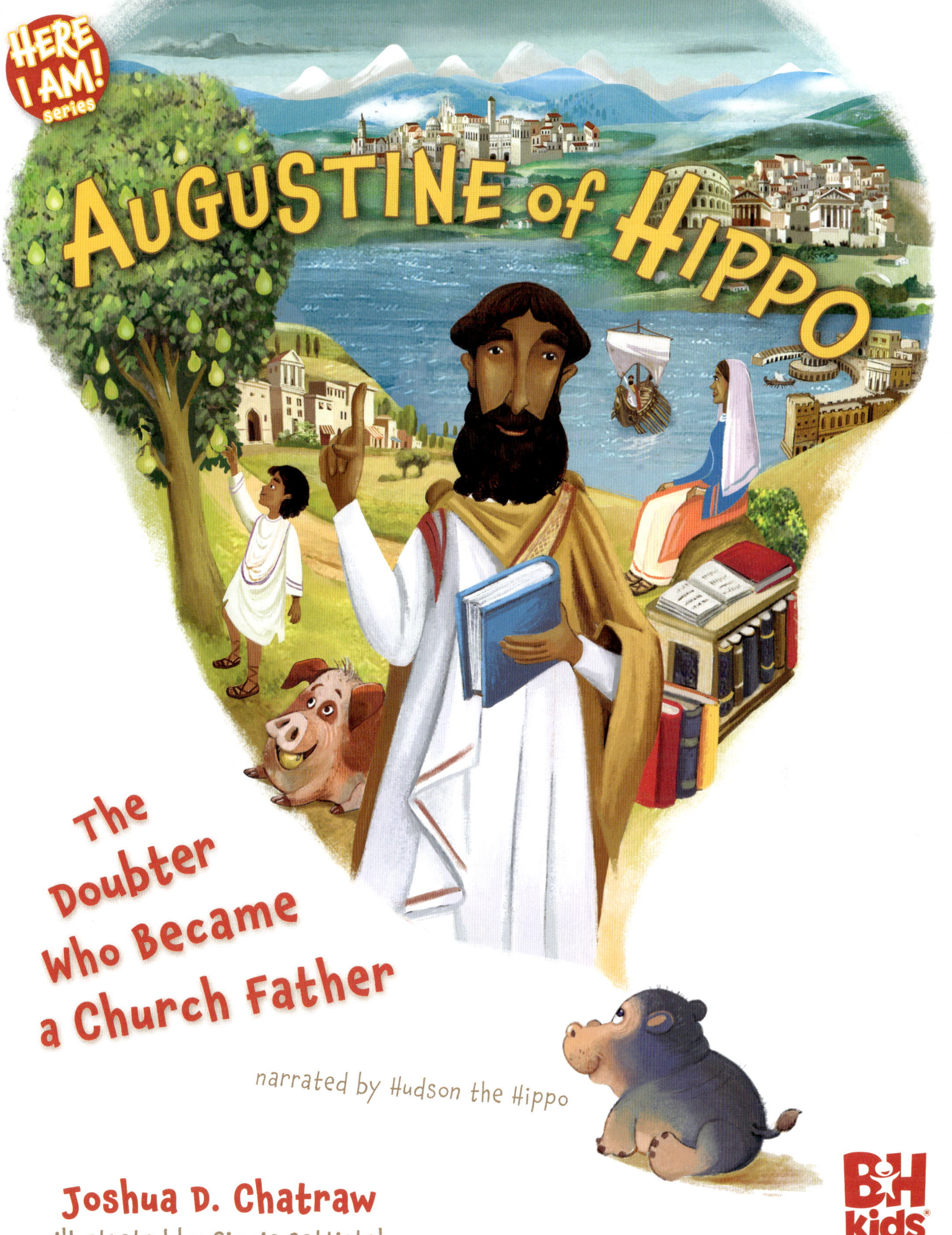


Joshua D. Chatraw
illustrated by Cinzia Battistel

B&H Kids
Brentwood TN

*For Addison and Hudson.*

*May your hearts rest in the Lord.*

979-83845-0590-7

Dewey Decimal Classification: CB
Subject Heading: AUGUSTINE, SAINT, BP. OF HIPPO \ CHRISTIANITY \ CHURCH
Printed in Shenzhen, Guangdong, China, December 2024
1 2 3 4 5 6 · 29 28 27 26 25

**Hi!**

My name is Hudson, and I have a story for you about a boy named Aurelius Augustinus. (That's a mouthful—even for a hippo!) He would grow up to be a great teacher, pastor, and writer known as Augustine of Hippo.

Augustine grew up in a time long before big screens, basketballs, or bikes. Yet in some ways, he wasn't much different from you. He went to school, played with his friends, and tried to please his parents.

Augustine's mom, Monica, was a Christian, but his dad wasn't. As a young boy, Augustine would go to church with his mom. But, like his dad, Augustine would soon begin to search for **everlasting love** in other places.

This was Augustine's big problem: He looked for everlasting love in all the wrong places. He loved God's gifts—things like school, games, and friends—as if they were the most important things. This made his heart restless.

***The harder we try to be happy our way instead of God's way, the more tired our hearts become.***

In school, Augustine's teachers taught him good things like reading, writing, and math, but they also gave him some wrong, **upside-down rules.**

Imagine that in soccer, you and your teammates are taught to kick the ball out of bounds instead of into the goal. You wouldn't believe someone who told you to aim for the goal because everyone around you played by these upside-down rules. That's like what happened to Augustine.

They taught Augustine that people can find everlasting love by being impressive—sounding cool, winning trophies, and being popular.

Augustine thought he was winning, but his heart still felt restless. The way his teachers taught him to "win" only left him tired, confused, and a long way from the love he was searching for.

Augustine tried to find love by impressing his friends. Once, he and his gang of friends stole some pears from a tree, although Augustine had better pears at home and wasn't even that hungry. He even threw some of the stolen fruit to nearby pigs.

*Have you ever been asked not to touch something, and then because you were told not to, only had an even stronger, unexplainable urge to touch it? This desire to disobey was part of why Augustine stole the pears. Can you think of people in the Bible who, for no good reason, disobeyed God and took a bite from some fruit?*

*No matter if it is Adam and Eve, Augustine, or you and me, we all have the same problem. Against good sense, we run away from everlasting love by disobeying God.*

With all his old teachers' lessons in mind, Augustine grew up and became known for his brilliant brain and his wonderful words. Back then, you didn't become rich and famous by dominating in sports or by singing to big crowds but by flattering people with fancy speeches.

His quest for fame led him to glittering cities, far away from home. With each move, Augustine's mom followed close behind, praying her son would find everlasting love in Jesus. But Augustine wanted to find love in **his own way.**
CARTHAGE
Once, he even snuck away from Monica on a ship.

Augustine's quest for love eventually led him to **Milan,** a city where grown-ups played by their own upside-down rules—chasing fun, fame, and fortune.

Augustine arrived thinking that all his dreams would come true. But his heart stayed achy and restless.

One day, Augustine went to church because he heard a pastor named Ambrose had a special way with words. While listening to Ambrose's sermons, he began to think more about the path to love his mom had long prayed for him to find.

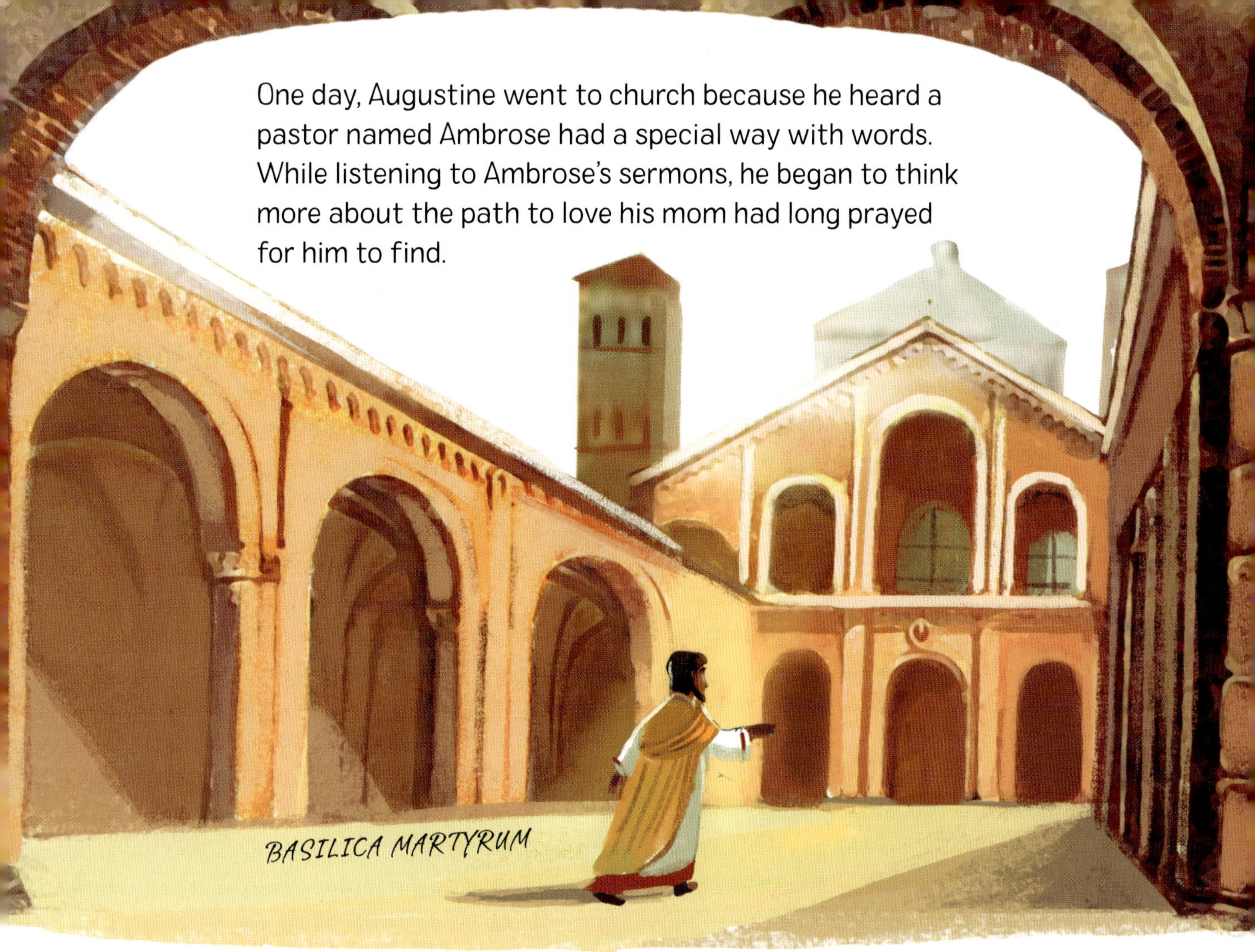

Maybe **Jesus** *was* the way to everlasting love.

Feeling tired and sad, Augustine found himself under another tree. This time, there were no pears or pigs, but there was a true friend named Alypius who, unlike the gang of friends from his childhood, was more concerned with loving Augustine than impressing him.
ALYPIUS

In tears, Augustine cried out to God for help. Suddenly, he heard a child's voice say, "Take up and read. Take up and read."

Augustine picked up a Bible and read the first verses he saw, part of which read: “Let us walk with decency . . . But put on the Lord Jesus Christ.” He didn’t need to read any further.

Even though Augustine had wandered far from God, he discovered Jesus as the way to God's **never-ending love.** Augustine had finally found the rest his heart was looking for.

Augustine's mom was overjoyed.
Her prayers had been answered.
Monica died in peace knowing that not only had Augustine become a Christian, but her husband, Patrick, had too.

Meanwhile, Augustine decided he was done chasing fame. He went away with his friends to live a quiet life thinking about God and talking about the Bible. But God had other plans.

News quickly spread that Augustine—who had made a name for himself with his dazzling words—was now making God's name known.

One day, on a trip to Hippo, people recognized Augustine and demanded he become their pastor. Even though this wasn't his plan, Augustine saw it as a **sign from God.**

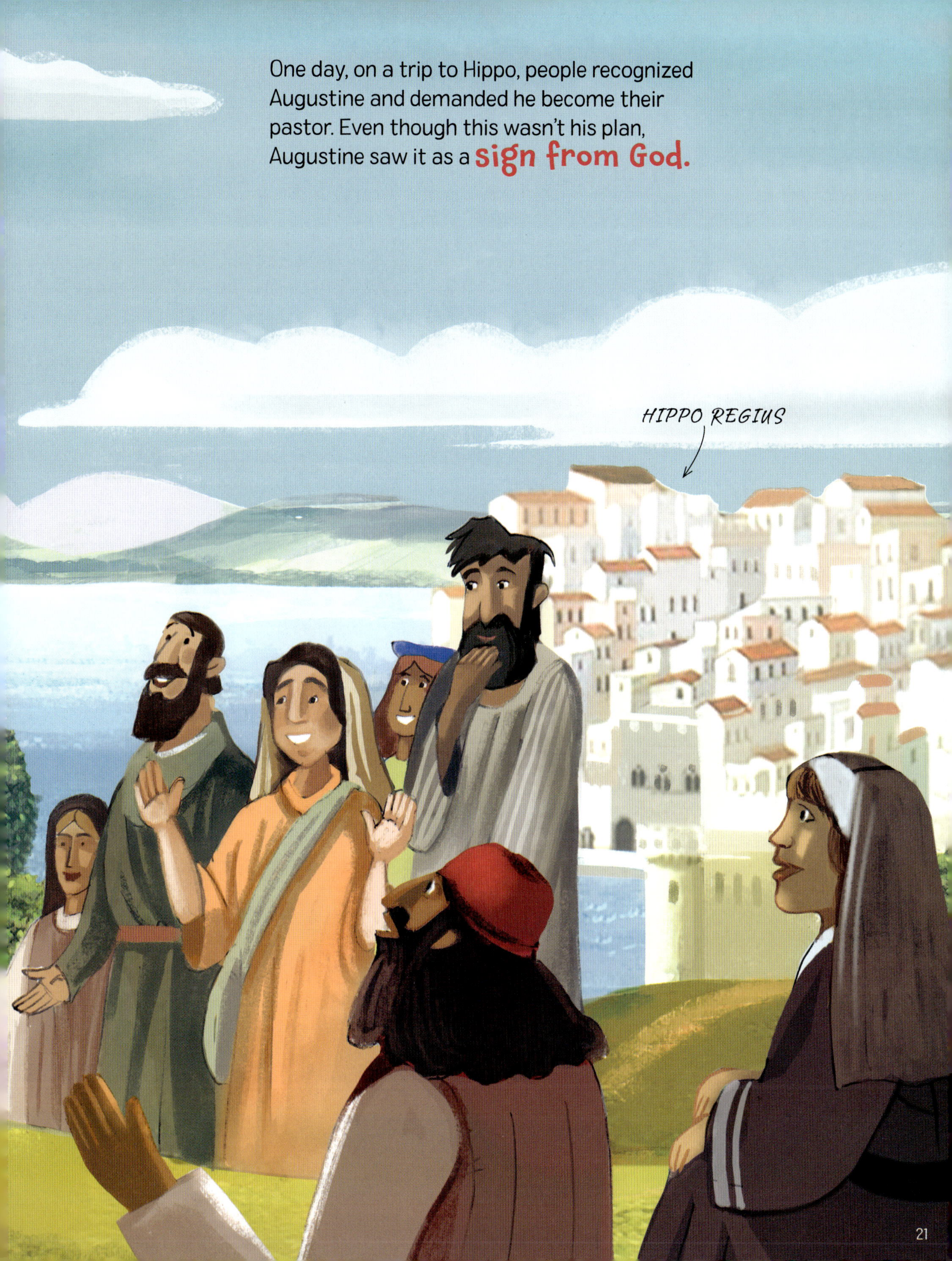

While Augustine was a pastor, he taught against the upside-down rules for life his teachers and friends had once taught him and helped people see that the way to **everlasting love** was by following Jesus.

Augustine also had to teach against false ideas confusing Christians within the church. He argued that since we are all born disobeying God, we can't earn His love. It can only be accepted as a gift.

Augustine also said that the church is like a hospital where spiritually sick people could begin to be healed and learn how to share the medicine of Jesus's love with the world.

False teachings in the church are called heresies.

Augustine saw how the upside-down rules he had once followed caused people not only to search for everlasting love in all the wrong places but also to treat people horribly.

He showed how Jesus's followers should live differently by fighting for the poor, freeing slaves, and caring for orphans.

Augustine also wrote many important books. In his most famous book, **Confessions**, Augustine wrote how his story was like Jesus's parable of the prodigal son, who left his home in search of love that only his father could give him.

As he ran from his dad's love, the son became miserable. Like young Augustine, the son in the parable also found himself with pigs!

In both stories, the lost son went down the wrong path, loving the father's stuff more than the father. In both stories, the son was welcomed back into everlasting love.

One of his most important books, **The City of God,** is the story of two cities: The earthly city is full of selfish and restless hearts; the city of God is filled with caring and joyful hearts.

Augustine wrote to invite people into God's eternal city—the only place with everlasting love.

*It took Augustine almost fifteen years to finish* **The City of God!**

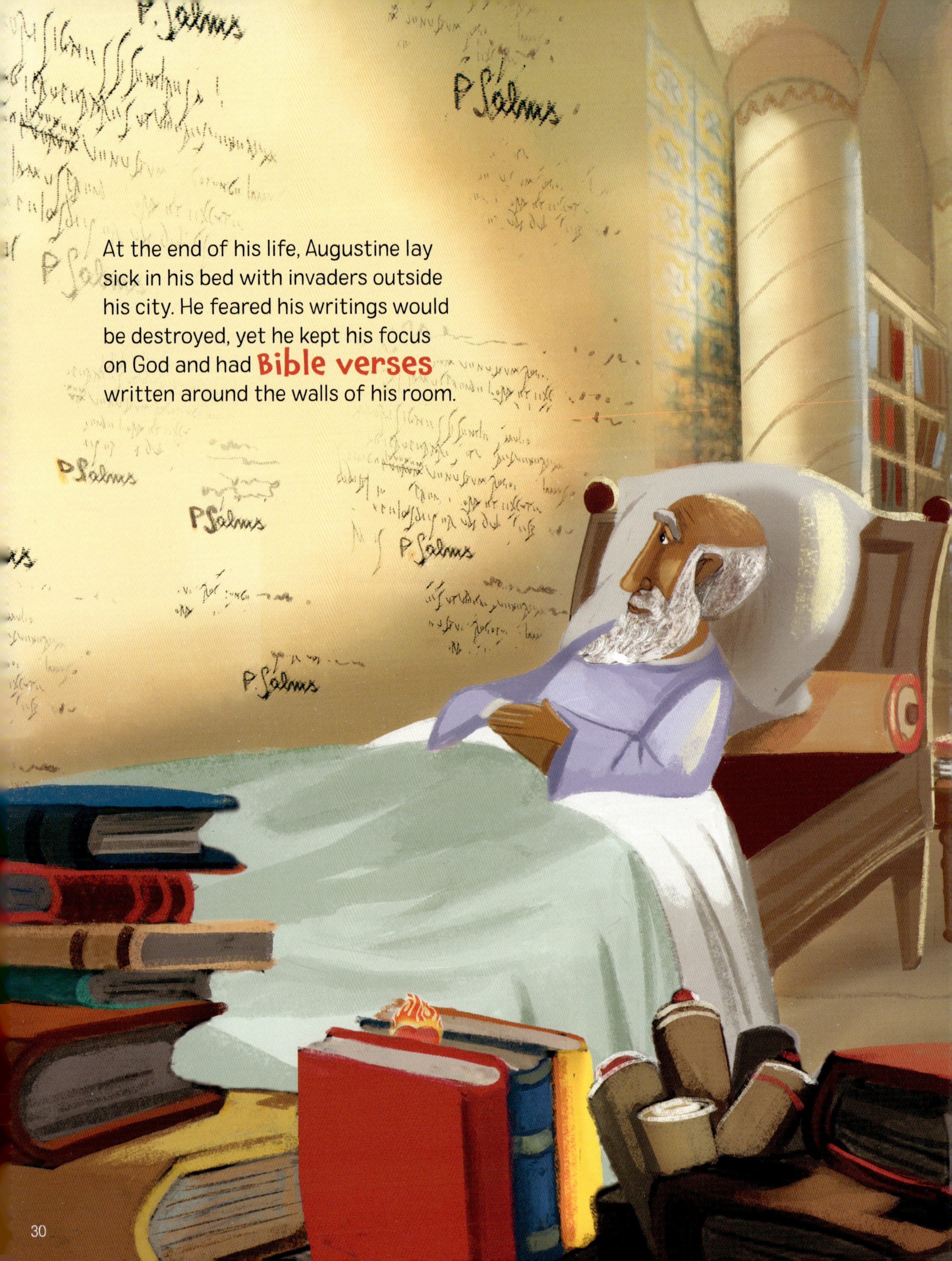

At the end of his life, Augustine lay sick in his bed with invaders outside his city. He feared his writings would be destroyed, yet he kept his focus on God and had **Bible verses** written around the walls of his room.

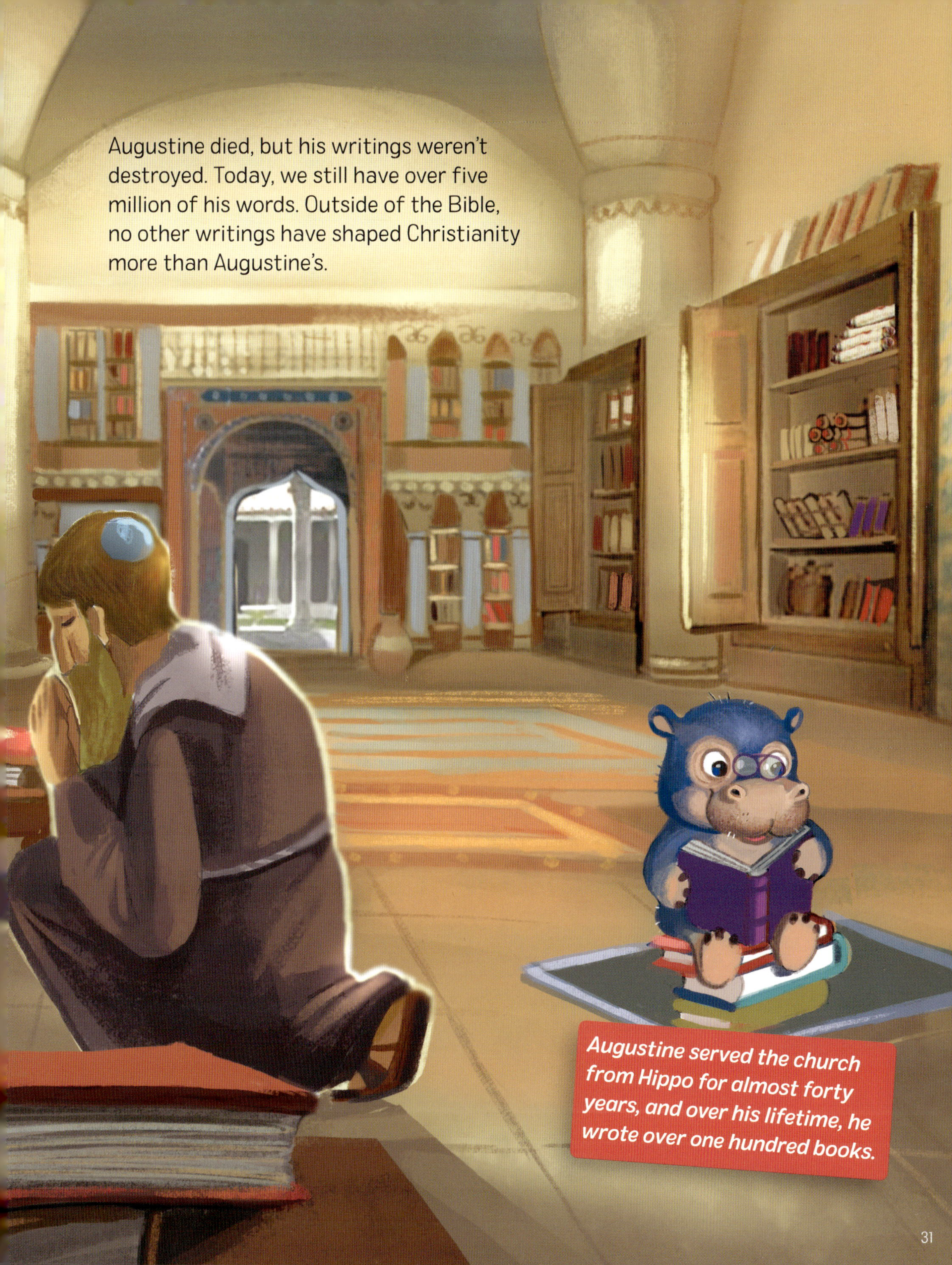

Augustine died, but his writings weren't destroyed. Today, we still have over five million of his words. Outside of the Bible, no other writings have shaped Christianity more than Augustine's.

*Augustine served the church from Hippo for almost forty years, and over his lifetime, he wrote over one hundred books.*

Augustine's most remembered words are from his prayer to God at the beginning of **Confessions:**